ORIGINS • ENDINGS

Poems

Ina Whitlock

for John

Also by the Author:

Eating the Chinese Pear
travelogue-memoir

Of Love and Loss
poetry

Sketches from Paraguaná
Venezuela, half a century ago

Stories of a Midwest Childhood
1930s–'40s

Published in the United States by
Spirit Journey Books, Vashon Island, Washington
iwhitlock@centurytel.net
www.InaWhitlock.com

ISBN: 978-0-9859929-1-0

Printed in the United States of America

Cover Art
"Interpretations" Watercolor by Ina Whitlock

I have many people to thank: my dear family and poetry loving friends, the poetry group readings of the last decade and more, and especially C. Hunter Davis and Eric Horsting for their critique. My thanks to Janice Randall for helpful prompting in word usage. I am grateful to all those wonderful and kind souls who have read and commented and given me suggestions and encouragement. From them I have learned much about the discipline and mystery of poetry. I am indebted to Jean Davies Okimoto for including poems of mine in her anthology, *The Weird World Rolls On.*

I thank Sy Novak of Novak Creative, Inc.,
for her design and print expertise, and especially,
I thank my editor, Nancy Morgan of Eagle Eye Editing,
for her technical help, her input and sharp eye,
that made the book possible.

CONTENTS

PERCEPTIONS

POWER

PROMPTINGS

DEPARTURES

BEGINNINGS

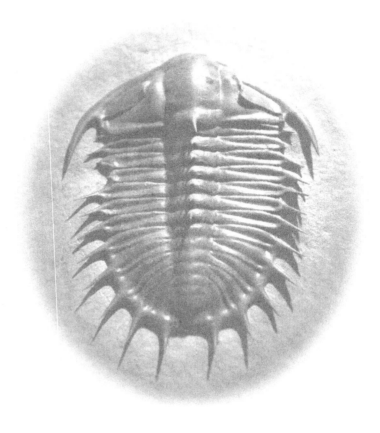

Trilobite

First member of all life forms,
Paleozoic inhabitant, progenitor
of mollusks, fishes, dinosaurs, the birds
—three-lobed creature, hard-shelled, surviving
three million years ruling oceans of Planet Earth
until the infinitely slow forces of evolution
and sudden global cooling climate change
made extinct five thousand orders of the genus
subphylum Schizoramia, save one, the marine
anthropod of today, retaining seventy-five percent
of Paleozoic body structure, records kept in stone:
Schizochoral lenses, angled planes (eyes like flies),
furrowed brow, glabella with pairs of sensory antennae,
smooth body, grooved thoracic segments
and fifteen jointed, paired limbs.

Trilobite beginnings five-hundred-fifty million
years ago, on a scale of time beyond imagining,
creatures scurrying sea beds, rolling in balls to escape,
threat response not unlike humanoids, we descendants
of deoxyribonucleic acid, and survivalists.

I am restored by a gift beyond millennia,
a pendant of the genus Calymene, one inch of oval stone
on a chain that mimics double spirals of DNA,
trilobite fossil alive in the wearing, the telling, as if
remembrance might restore endurance,
substance at the core, the spine
of everyday living.

2010

Earth Matrix

Man, I've pulled you from dark waters,
from cold escarpments of amoebic pasts
to warm you on gold-orbed diluvian dawns.

I am the land on which you feed,
the valleys where your passions flow,
dark loam you plow into tomorrows
that my fecundity gives birth.

You scrape shards of history,
plant continental fields with flags,
then on tidal waves of night return
to drop your flaming harvests down,

Sky fires that sear death from life,
and when you fall, I plant your atoms deep
within the matrix of all possibility.

Zoomorphic Message

I've dug you up,
exposed you to the light
with other bits,
a frog's head and a shard,
but they seem mute,
you've motion there to speak
on that chipped mouth,
my small bird/man.

You are not much, the site
is long ignored.
You do not stand alone
but as a leg of larger ware,
a ceremonial pot
for the long dead.

Your eyes—so strange—
made of three coils of clay
can look all ways.
The quizzical effect
unsettles me.

What faculty of art lets me
forget the archaeology
and lets you speak
across eight centuries?
No ciphered word
or language primitive,
but underneath my skin
a message strikes directly—
the ancient potter's wit.

1960s, Aruba

Clan

Born into, but not of—clan,
surround of infant skin responds
to tribal drums, a quickening of
deep rivers trailing dreams.

Dance of light and sound,
shadows on tent or wall,
illusions of windsong incised
in rhyme and stone.

Cuneiform and alphabet,
history of shield and spear,
text of moon, sky, stars, entangled
quantum, cyber, fractal fields.

Diasporas of memory,
in the unending chant,
the flutter of the yet unborn
entering the clan of Planet Earth.

2010

Machu Picchu

Manco Capac, Inca, Son of The Great Sun:
Now I know why your descendants
Climbed to heights where mists were rolling,
Worshiped at the gateway of the world
The Sun above all else,
For I stood in your most Holy Place
And your god came out to greet us
Though I had my plastic raincoat on.

We climbed Inca's Citadel,
Stone on numbered stone,
All two thousand and one steps,
Awed by narrow terraces that held us
From ramparts precipitous that fall
Six thousand feet, and we heard below
The Urubamba River roar.

City hidden when the fourteenth
Of a line-recorded Dynasty
Fled Spanish Conquerors,
Conquered alone, in death and rubble,
Lost four hundred years from maps
—With thirty-seven thousand acres
Of the Southern Hemisphere—found,
We uttered, "Fantastic!"

Machu Picchu, Heart of Inca,
Heart of Death and Living,
A presence in grey mists obscuring
All but your high altar, where food
For The Sun was left on five low steps
Carved in one stone, and we sat down
And ate our lunch, not reverently enough.

Manco Capac, Inca, Son of The Great Sun:
Standing at the crest of your lost world—
Tourists waiting for a bus to take us down
—Your Sun showed favor, let us see
Entirety in one great sweep,
Matching man's and nature's greatness
All in one, and I thought I'd never be the same,
But a lady from Ohio was discussing a bug spray.

1968, Peru

Flight

River stream in canyons far below,
sweepings of snow on steeps,
volcanic stones, abrasions deep
in dusk at twenty thousand feet.

Rising on wings of waning light,
an infinite indigo of intent
to find unearthly realms—
in thrall of cosmic beginnings.

Fusion of galaxy and molecule,
what mind creation possible
in the surging, inward-outward throb,
the probe of wing's strobe light?

Then glide to earth, return, sentient
in desire to arrive, and know.

ENCOUNTERS

Mood Mountain

Bronzed blade of sun at her side,
God Vulcan sculpted her body
by wind and snow, each crevasse exposed.

Volcanic plumes arose to form her,
small quakes convulse in seismic
magnitude, and dull clouds shower

Her moods, or gage the weather,
announcing the earthly presence of
Beautiful Tahoma, wife of Mt. Olympus.

Blamed for sloth and banished
to far Cascadian shore, she carries
a papoose on northern shoulder.

Towns gather at her sacred skirts.
She is crowned in dolphin clouds
or hidden under grey umbrellas.

Renamed, Rain-near, Rain-here,
Mt. Rainier surprises at 8 a.m.
in salmon-colored sky.

Afternoon, she wears velvet white,
or veil of pollution, boa of smog,
half the vision of her prime.

With rising temperature, sleeps late.
Cancels performance if guests arrive.
We are blessed by any greeting

Or fair evening's benediction
if she appears in full snow-dress,
blushing in sun's last caress.

Hey Boys

Hey boys, with pink cheeks, smiles,
   on a dusty road of mountainside,
   chiming a chorus of 'hellos'
   through windows of our tourist car,
   your faces full of curiosity,
   captivating rag-tag kids entwined,
   growing up together, clowning
   like beautiful children, anywhere.
   But you were in the sun-washed,
crystal air of Kashmir.

Was I naïf to think that I could know
   anything about you—forgotten, until
   a photo fell from a book—and now
   I wonder what has happened to you.
   If you played in fabled gardens,
   or blizzard storms of politics.
   If time has dulled the beauty of Lake Dal,
   the classic patterns, or tapestry
   of Srinegar in a causal tide of years.
Hey boys—where are you now?

2012

The Box

Under medallioned lid
a few shells and a stone.
What can be said for these
seined long ago by her hand
from sands of the Yellow Sea?

Small whelks surround
a tri-shaped rock, capturing
dark fossil ferns
and flowers so small,
so delicate, to have survived.

Endurance through eons,
stone surface smoothed
by fire, ice, sea—earth's
adornments thrust forth
to mingle with this day.

Dark history in a wooden box.
Embossments on the lid,
dull copper-winged bats
in four corners guard
from a pilfering hand.

Under lid, surprise! A 1930s
postal stamp—a face,
Generalissimo Chiang Kai-shek,
his green cap frayed,
Mandarin script and number five.

Here, two histories conspire:
American, her enchantment
to learn, become other—then
army conquering—chaos,
occupation, separation, gone.

Surge of remembrance
from the Yellow Sea—
affinity of gatherer and gift—
her affirming hand
on a note—"Tsingtao, China."

2005

Crow Mother

Punctuations of crow alphabet
  on a green field, the clan, alarmist,
    crabbing when I stop and stare.

Black empiricists, scavengers,
  omnivorous, raucous, rowdy,
    come together conversing,
spreading alarm—and I think, if I stay,
  will they all fly away?

One by one, then pairs, they leave
  squawking—yet a few remain
    crow resolute, until the clan chief
flies, and my surety of self also.
  Am I so easy to dissuade

After a moment's pleasantness,
  taking flight from greenest fields
    to forage hinterlands, abandoning
intent in flights of fancy,
  following whims of others?

Or am I, like ancient Crow Mother,
  watching them fly, before I go?

2010

Peonies and Rusted Truck

Peonies explode in flame

      knife to the heart of fear
           slide of a truck in rain

      slight distance between us

phantom driver into the brush
      burning underside

         we—free

    but mirage
        of the rusted truck

      stays.

Jo Anne

You appear clearly, a sudden
picture over my right shoulder,
blond-red hair falling to your shoulders,
knowing the weight of the world,
holding your share of what was given
in life, at twenty-nine, or so.

You walk through tower doors
but cannot keep your world
from crashing downward, down,
taking skin and crushing bones,
your long hair aflame.

Jo Anne, I don't know you
or what you lived, but your name
comes again, and the face,
hair frazzled and singed,
nylons smooth on sturdy legs
learning to walk at an early age.

From where, the Midwest, Omaha?
You have the look, but impossible
(when I check a victims' manifest)
to know why your footsteps led
to hard streets of New York.

Jo Anne, you were the one
of thousands, to gather my tears
before your spirit-body disappeared.
The one to know when darkness falls,
The Light, and yours
the last word, "Murderers!"

11 September 2001, Cape Breton

Anchored to Earth

On this calm, rock-rimmed shore
how can I comprehend
terror a thousand miles away?
How find my world of ill intent
when an ever-flowing lake
denies all else, but this respite—
a beautiful place and day?

Here, calm waters swill the stones
and slake my thirst for peace,
yet, I can hear them scream—the lucky ones—
stunned and bloody, running through debris.
Unfathomable the numbers, who they were—
did not escape the happenstance of fate
when bright morning was drawn to dark.

What thoughts, what dreams
burned on entering a rage of fire—
Hell's bolts of Armageddon—
while on my ageless, rock-rimmed shore,
a sparrow sings in the scrag of a tree?

11 September 2001, Cape Breton

Mortal Beauty

In stark steel of waiting room
oblique light falls on a face,
a marble Michelangelo's
David, but lying on his back,
dressed in ski clothes, ski boots
that reach beyond the edge
of a gurney as they wheel him in.

I grab for a lifeline in the chill
of a fragile moment that shatters
the surface of efficiency
in this dark room, where time
reels a slow line, as we wait,
we are waiting, and I've only
fallen on ice for a broken arm.

Who attends you, David, Adonis, Per?
Have loved ones been informed?
I long to stand by you, to find
a lover's gaze in the color of your eyes,
fathom life's mysteries there,
but your beauty lies in solemn sleep
and my arm hurts too much to move.

At last, a man in black ski clothes,
your witness (or rescuer?)
comes exchanging brisk words
in Norsk, with a noncommittal nurse.
They depart, leaving us here, and I
with no clue for my anxious heart.

Nordic light falls on your form.
You are too far away for me to know
if breath rises under a sky-blue jacket
bringing—like dawn into the room—
effulgent news of life, and I'm
unwilling to conclude that mortal
beauty should so soon turn to stone.

1984, Norway

SOUNDINGS

Swimmers

Up there—
    clouds, a marbled musculature
        of arms plowing eternal waves.
        Down here—
            we swim for dear life.

River Run

With fierce agility the river
    runs deep, a swirl of mystery
    in timeless flow beyond
    earth's impediments,
        past word, past dream.

Magic

Unearthly appearance at dawn—
  dew-diamonded wings,
    silvery, translucent threads
    spun on a sea of grass.
Shipwrecked angels, ethereal
  adventurers marooned
    until daylight, when suddenly,
      they've sailed away
without my knowing
  if funnel web
    or ghostly butterflies
      have brought their magic here.

Cape Breton

Swallows

How swallows love the fog—
    swooping playful schools,
      minnows in sky's grey pool,
        sudden—gone, come again,
      winged flocks in pirouette,
      shirring tops of trees, audacious,
Giving edge to this day.

Farewell

Sadness lingers under canopy
of Ironwood's brittle shroud;
first light, through scraggly limbs
filters a scrunch of needles underfoot,
where I search for you, the missing one.

Ironwood's underworld of Kauai,
where night violence of machete
split the hoary husk of coconut's sweet flesh,
the honeycreeper sips, sucks, tweets
a bacchanal of Glorias in gelatinous mess.

Dawn brushes the red/ochre earth
and sun paints in plaintive splendor
grief's distraught fire with exuberant light,
lifting death from Ironwood's shelter,
as a bird sings the island alive again.

2003, Kauai

Bosque Las Trucas

In solitude the forest sings
    but not alone—
      a trembling breeze
    lifts leafy darkness
      to a generosity of light,
    then falls in glissandos
      on a dappling stream.

2008, Chile

Magic Eyes

In a thicket of ivy—jewels of flashing fire—
surprise in dewed leaves, winking eyes,
gems of red and yellow, sporadic stares,
dewdrops that disappear
in whispers
of wind.

2010

Clamshells

Northwestern tide crochets
a shawl in watery glaze
of limpets, pebbles, sands
awash in surging songs,
the arias of life and love
and death—clamshells,
one held high, the other
at her waist, Carmen
dances with castanets.

Flute

Phrase lingering,
  a mellifluous
  flow of melody
  released from score
  by crimson lips,
  andante's breath,
  deft fingertips,
  a silver wand
  on agile wings,
  love's theme
  inseparable
  from body's sway
  or lift of arm,
  mood's melody,
  refrain, return,
  resolve of capriccio
  and toccata, dancing
  through the hall,
binding all audience
  in applause.

2008

Sitar Transits

Sound strange
  to the Caucasian ear—
  a yowling, atonal spin
  of wired strokes
  impaling air,
  scrawling decibels
  reverberating
  in seductive theme—
  the sudden earthy jabs
  of tabla in player's hands,
  dark-eyed entrancement
  of ethereal spheres,
  disparate voices entwined
  in aria and masculine reply,
  a spiraling continuum,
  a dervish physicality
  until release,
  in one last
  note.

Quartet on a Theme
of Shostakovich

From where—Dresden—this deep brooding
   strike on cities of my mind, music
      thrust by bow across the ribs,
         spirals of hurt sounding

through chambers of my heart, the strings'
   gut searing resonance, in dark recess
      where utmost sorrow springs,
         loosened from decades, centuries,

cloistered chains of minds—beyond all music—
   that inflict not sweetly, nor from glory
      but the gall of human failing—
         a dissonance the quartet plays,

yet sustains, in such tenderness
   the sacred sounds of suffering,
      humankind's music for remembering—
         the ultimate, enduring tone.

2010

Mandarin Archive

Sound my language cannot speak,
mordant music, thin
yet full in depth, a quick alteration
of tone, a tender, tearful flow,
sad, lonely, yet beautiful
song of memory so deep,
a world unknown to me—
your childhood and your script.

Discordance of crumpled lines,
notation from a numbered score,
wail of weird instruments
rushing from the past into this now.
Classic Chinese music on CD,
strangeness of your boyhood heard,
seeking solidity where there is none,
nor any hope of seeing you again.

With sounds of dizi, erhu, pipa,
emboldened decibels and arcing bows,
my deaf western ears, unaccustomed
to sudden shifts, or tap of clanging gongs
that strike an hour on timeless wing
of song—Mandarin remembrance,
pervasive reeds, flute rushing to a lake
where the Dowager Empress waits.

Sweet-bitter tune; flowering lotus
shivers on sibilant breeze
of "Spring on Moonlit River"
and "Moon on Mirrored Pond."
What loves transpired, transcend
a rustle of silk, or sword—
sustain the music's subtle change,
never returning the same?

You—Little White Devil—
child born in Peking,
singing rote lessons of school,
shuffling a path by the moat and wall
of old Nan Suchow, and I hear
in a song what I'd not known before,
your sad singularity—my worldly
body shaken, as if you were here.

DREAMS

Shambler's Song

I'm a shambler searching for a face
to match the flecks upon a mirror,
a photograph to make life real.
A shutter snaps within my mind
as shapes impinge upon the sun
and unaccomplished gestures are
the precious possibility,
the backdrop of my scenery.

I rim the highest peaks and whirl
toward the spheres or dive below
the deepest seas to find what's real,
or burst in flames of night that fade
in morning's glare on sheets of snow,
a place where plastic roses grow.

I walk the streets of small despairs
and mark an X on playground walls,
but can't erase nonentity
from crumbling bricks of a lost time,
yet I come back in varied clothes
a techni-scene and colored hair
and wonder yet, what role I'll find
on the screen within my mind.

1960s

Sea Woman

Sea woman drifts from a usual day
  ignoring chipped cups in a sink
    as soapsuds rise in spume
      and sea breeze combs her hair.

Searching the golden curves of sand
  for luster of agate, secret of shells,
    she dances with gulls on wind-lifted wings,
      sings to a chorus of waves' dull thud.

Her bones are the wind-washed frame,
  shack of a fishmonger's wife
    who serves anemones in rusting cans,
      seines starfish with silver nets

That she weaves to tell her stories—
  at sea's edge, where old women endlessly
    crochet rivulets of waves
      to seam the earth and sea together.

Unwinding seaweed from her hair,
  she reaches with sandy foot a shoe
    under driftwood decay of the kitchen table
      —knows she will go to the sea again.

1970s

Legions of Light

Strange evening,
  when diaphanous glints
of underworld skitter
  like phosphorescent eels
on coastal waterline,

Legions invading
  north to south, Neptune
in command,
  if no moon holds sword
on Puget Sound.

2004

Micmac

Entering deep woods
where light and shadow
play dark games
on rootage, lichen, loam,
I'm not alone.

Wind murmurs myth
in pine boughs and I
follow footprints down
through ragged ferns
that sealskin leggings part.

Proud Micmacs,
carrying birch canoes,
at lakeside disappear.

Cape Breton

The Object and The Search

Why suddenly I went outside
when all the dinner guests were just at hand,
or why I was compelled
to get binoculars—but then, I did.

The view was all too clear of the peninsula
across some fifteen miles of sea, and mountains
cut a jagged edge into the sky where
two new promontories—never seen before—
far to the east, were clear, the view
was better than any past evening's watch.

I don't know why, but then I saw—
not knowing—what I'd hoped to see,
mistook it for a lighthouse
on that peninsula where once we'd gone,
and if it had been clear the day we climbed
the stairs to those six pie-shaped rooms,
I might have seen myself as coming here
across the miles and years, but when I looked,
the lighthouse was not there,
and I remembered it was not white and red,
but wind-washed wood.

I thought it was a buoy, quite far at sea,
not in water—exactly—and tried to focus
with naked eye, the whirling silvery thing
traveling at great speed
until it disappeared in a rain squall, and I
went in to dinner and the guests,
feeling guilty then, for wanting to see,
after I did, and not able to say.

1960s, Aruba

Drift of a Student at Sea

As you settled into porch chairs
  on the drift of a warm afternoon,
I was at sea taking measurements
  and forgot to look ashore.
Slower than dreams, the abstractions
  got out of hand—like the oars,
but I didn't shout, I was looking on
  like you with your binoculars.

On a yellow raft, floating
  away from your emerald shore,
I'd lost all papers overboard
  though I had a survival kit
and a patch box handy as a mirror,
  but the sun fell too fast on my scheme.

When lights came on in town
  I knew that you were there
on the uncommitted side,
  gathered on the safety of the shore
having heard that I was missing,
  a luminosity of eyes
staring into a dark sea, as if you
  had suspended living too.

Was my reflection in the stars?
  My image drowned in morning light?
Did you send rescue, make life visible,
  or was the word 'Expendable'
between my eyes? I'd never
  felt such weight before, but now—
the only evidence is drift.

1960s, Aruba

Northern Shore

Glacial outcroppings form
   a narrow field of stones,
   mutable, transformed
   by fire and ice,
   shadowed, sunbathed,
   in shifting waves
   singing earth's heartbeat.

Cape Breton

Quiet

Uncharted hills and valleys
  shimmer where our lives together
   form broad fields
and nocturnal music is heard
  in afterglow beyond
a golden aura on earth's ridge
  where the spine, the body of our lives
lies closed, and shall remain
  in unwritten wonderment.

PERCEPTIONS

Old Familiar

I had forgotten how the scent
    of fresh baked cookies
cheers a house, brings the old
    sweet, familiar entering
on wafts of clove and cinnamon,
    crisp morsels, a kiss
        of memory.

2013

Postcards to Myself

Stamped in first light's memory,
dark elms, vacant sky.
Nebraska's timelessness,
grey room and rocking chair,
a grandmother's enfolding arms.

Drought nights hot, sleeping out
under stars on army cot.
Dried grass sharp under foot,
alley paving burns,
a cement basement floor,
cool, dark, smooth
for dancing tippy-toe.

Wind-up phonograph with horn.
Thomas A. Edison's barking dog.
Fit a needle in the groove,
"Hungarian Rhapsody #2"
or "Glow Worm" in twirling tune.

Ennui of summer days, surprised
by monoplane writing the sky,
or playing paper dolls, my favorite
Rosalie, the dark-haired beauty,
bridesmaid of the bride.

Clusters of tiny bouquets,
in Spiraea's hideaway,
where sun flakes cut through shade
in a bower of lost time,
and I hoped, wanted, waited,
until of age to know the way
of school, the words.

Jack Benny Sundays

Too numerous to recall
all but the sound of the voice
and the squeak of Jack's violin
playing sound waves of radio
with a twist of the dial on the old
wooden console—a half hour
of Jack Benny at 7 o'clock.

Jack, and his Mary Livingstone
refuting the whine and the pessimist's
ploy, all played for laughs
meant for better days than silences
in 1930s depression greys.

Jack and his droll valet, Rochester,
rendering verdict on his skinflint,
cantankerous boss, who once
at the point of a gun, in hesitation,
when the robber asks, "Your money
or your life?"—has to think it over.

Sundays after Sunday School,
a cafeteria meal, or summer treat
—The Big Apple—a Red Delicious
apple-shaped drive-in dispensing
through big teeth, a cherry coke
and hamburger, and I'm in
the back of a '34 Ford coupe.

Long drive past a cemetery
to a modest bungalow, unless
on special Sundays, to the zoo
and the monkeys' feeding time,
dressed in sunsuits, a boy and girl,
sitting at a kid's table, with bowls
and spoons, eating mashed bananas.
"Your cousins," my dad said.

Or Pioneers Park for a picnic,
where the bronze buffalo stands
and a towering Sioux brave
sends messages by blanket and smoke
across a vast Nebraska plain.

Summer sightings of biplanes,
or a dirigible, filled eyes with
20th century wonders in an age
when a nation of patriots gathered
by radios on Sunday night, for the
comic send-up of ordinary man.

What not to listen for? Silly dilemmas,
one-line solutions for penny-pinching
vanity, the always to be 39 Jack,
the rasp of his violin, jokes solvable
and understood in an adult world,
so simple, my childhood thoughts
at the final "We're a little late,
so good-night folks—"
Best half hours I had with my dad.

2010

Home Where

Beyond an airport's windowpane
a freeway and three signs,
Sioux City, St. Paul, Lincoln.
I've come too far aligning roads,
connecting turns in Minneapolis
Airport corridors, the forgotten
Midwest twang and travelers'
small talk, feeling that the sod
might rise to meet my bones,
replant me once again in youth.

Minnesota, Iowa, Nebraska born.
These flat lands were all I knew;
a farm and forest lakes, a family
and yesterdays' dry winds,
drought, fragments of cracked earth,
a puzzle of Nebraska soil and soul,
a stubborn forgetfulness—
anathema to prairie pride—
memory weathering dust and loss.

Airport transit—leaving soon as I
arrive, as if such places never
seeped into my being, or have I
come too far, too many continents
to know where is home, but everywhere,
no destination, a connecting flight
to Lincoln and the loss—a stranger
to the girl I was.

2004

Clothesline

Sweet breeze of cleanly things
sweeps Northwest grey rain away
so errant flags of socks and sleeves
can wave and moist sheets fly
across a cerulean bed of sky.

Squinting into sun, I clip
fresh washed laundry up,
remembering clothespins too high
to paint round dolly faces on
—in Midwest memory.

Lines of baby clothes hung stiff
in Northeast storms, a spin of years
with Automatic Wash and Dry
until today's return to line
and clothes' backyard embellishment
in mid-day colors' fine display,
my pleasure in the simple task.

2008

Housework

Housework is everything I'd rather not,
an endlessly accumulating list I've got,
like rotting garbage, hard to carry out.
A need, unless my wisely cultivated creed
describes the dozen cobwebs in a room
as beautiful, no cause to raise a broom
in jousting rafters, knacking beams.

Doña Quixote in sweat pants, dreams
while swiping rude outcroppings of grime
accumulated—with good intentions—over time.

Housewife in frustration mode,
unless involved in syntactic code,
releases creative wiles in dramatic episode
while tangling self in vacuum cleaner cord,
attempting rescue of boiled-dry kettle
from amalgamation of burner on red-hot metal.

Guilty and humbled, with no heart for tea,
in varied states, out of harmony
with housework—or any like kind—
proving good results are hard to find.

So work? I like my messy home.
Paint my pictures, write my poem.

1962

55

MacNeil's Cat

The old house is down that Jakie built
on a veteran's pension in '46, the place
on a hill, where the porch floundered
like a ship's prow in Cape Breton storms.

Four bedrooms up, nine windowpanes
and none the same, the house where
Jakie's wife raised bread and nine kids
and Jakie went down in the mines

To keep them alive, stayed on
'til his lungs did not keep pace
with a lack of oxygen, his life in a drift
of coal dust and cigarettes.

And there was squabbling and loss
when fair Eileen went down in the grave
and Jakie struck the fourth son lame.
A history only crows tell now.

Before we tore the old place down,
Jakie said, "Look for the 1946 penny
I put by the window frame,
notched in a two-by four."

And I promised I would, but wondered
just how lucky that penny was.
And it wasn't long 'til MacNeil's cat
ground up the hill, MacNeil in control,

A demolition master, and with just one
strike of the dozer bucket, caught
the old place in the rib, cracking,
with a grunt and groan of old bones.

Loud purr of incessant treads
as the cat rocked back, then hit again,
breaking windows' blank stare
in a requiem of glass shattering.

Motorized distortions brought down
beams with a twist and a moan,
compressing to sighs, the hardboards
bought cheap on a miner's pay.

Jakie's place, gone from the hill—
the shredded raw fibers of fifty years—
the labor, the pain, and poverty of lives
left a hole in the sky, and a penny lost.

1993, Cape Breton

The Gift

In fullness of the gift of love
—broccoli—planted by your hands,
my farmer son, a gesture measured
in two rows of pale teal leaves,
stalks strong, leaf sheaths, nubs,
brassica florets to grow
from earth's fecund effluvium
in the apex between birth and death
—of seed and bolted flower—
broccoli, a gift of nourishment,
and love's soul sustenance.

2009

My Old Garden

My old garden,
my lookout, hangout, treasure
of imminent surprise
and careless ease, where I tread lightly
not to disturb any gift that might come up
on its own; a forgotten bulb,
a wandering seed or disguised weed,
will get no help, or hindrance from me,
yet bring magic to a wayside hill too steep
to manicure, too hazardous to climb.

Below, in golden spring, long strands
of willow sway, as if a young girl's hair
is brushed by breeze, and summer's willow
weeps over a sunny court of visitors.

My rain-soaked, wrinkle-leaved,
patchy quilt of garden on clay mud bank
rewards me, even at its January worst,
dazzles, when late sun paints silver on
ferns' sprawl over rock retaining wall.

Rose hips of the poorly pruned rose
hint of seductive abundance in May,
blush-colored petals and sensual sniffs.
Tags of last season's Red Rhodies,
deadheads of hydrangea, I should have cut
before a warm day brought baby buds.

Stripped stalks of raspberry at the upper wall
await attention of glorious, summer days.
Berries, buds, and bulbs, I tend you
not enough, grateful only that you come up
from under dead grass, crumpled leaves
of garden's winter blankets in the rain—
to magnify sun's rare February day.

Espaliered peach of fifty years,
brutally pruned, and my long wait
for a thumb's bruise, to pluck down,
taste succulence under red-fuzz skin.

Oh, rosemary and oregano, blessing
our meals all year, partners in surround
of motley greens and browns;
old cherry suckers heading for the sky,
ugliness redeemed but once a year
when April's snow blossoms fall,
and the tea rose near the porch rail
flairs outward, ten feet wide,
tangling in willow's hair.

Twin cedars anchor this house to a hill,
guarding a nest of white clamshells
at cedars' root, on a sacred hillside
where Salish buried obsidian.
My eyes toil over this scene
of what is lost, past possibility
in this garden of careless ease,
this jungle of neglect—and my felicity.

1987

Blackberry Time

Here, again,
    on this beach, where memory
    is gain of years, and blackberries
    pace the season of indulgence
    and work, picking the ripe
    from an untimely pluck,
    by a soft squeeze of the dark
    sweet globules, savoring
    in wisdom and luck, the recall
    and endeavor, not stretching too far
    —or balance lost to thorns,
    torturous vines, scratched veins,
    blackberry stains, caught—
Caught again!

Intruder

You've been in for a few days.
  How can I let you out
    into a cold rain

In your delicate, waning state
  when time draws to winter—
    in this foreign territory

Of my warm living room—
  not your promised land?
    Though somehow,

A few days ago, you found
  your way and something
    strange fluttered my eyes.

On close examination
  I had to wonder why
    you landed

On the armature
  of Mother's old brass lamp,
    still surviving

In the living room, far from
  a winter sepulcher outdoors,
    finding shelter,

Fragile beauty, pale wings yellow,
  a cut of black on wingtip—
    extraordinary in November,

Alone, and I also,
  taking pleasure that you
    came into my vision

On lamp, chair leg, or floor,
  urchin, with wings spread
    as if for flight.

No place to go, so you stay,
  wings in subtle movement
    as if breathing, you survive

until the night,
  on a drop of honey caught,
    you die before morning.

I can't even dream how
  you got indoors through doors,
    your presence a gift

      of wonderment,
        entrapment,
        and loss.

2012

Croak On

Croak on, old frog,
   the white butterfly
      flutters away.

Sounds of
   your comic song
      end summer's day,

Soften earth's burnt edge
   where roots and timbers die
      and leaves not gathered

Rot in fetid pools,
   harboring no seasons
      or solace to survive

Unless we waken
   to millennial songs—
      so croak on, old frog,

Conjure the birds
   from silences;
      a prince to kiss

The white butterfly
   of truth and beauty,
      so fragile, so fleeting.

Croak on, old frog,
   reveal the folly of
      forgetful men.

2009

POWER

Man Power

My grandfather carried a rifle
into the snowy fields,
shot a buck and tagged it,
permit for winter meals.

Now meat is wrapped in plastic,
no blood, gore, or ritual,
no drastic act is seen.

Eyes are on a target—"them."
Replay of old war games;
to shoot from hip, ship, sky,
and reap tagged body bags.

My grandfather's father came
to the U.S.A.
to avoid the killing fields.

When a child, I gathered twigs
to 'shoot 'em up' at the OK Corral.
Now, handguns are allowed
in parks where children play.

2009

The Game

Arrogant and ignorant, they say
we North Americans—
Stars and Stripes unfurled,
flap wrapping 'round the world.

Warring eagles overhead
turn heavens black and red—
rockets' awesome display
like a Fourth of July
gone bad in Baghdad.

American soldier takes aim
as a boy runs toward him
with a grenade cradled
in his arms like a puppy or toy.

Whom can we blame?
A soldier unable to forget
an arabesque of blood
staining desert sand
with lost history of a child?

Blame the body politic,
governmental cogs that turn
Peace into War, not knowing
any language but its own?

Rules and places change,
but killing stays the same
when death is avenged
in worship of the battlefield,
and blind perversion calls

Death and destruction victory,
yet only when we perceive
all children as our own, will we
win the game called Peace.

2002

A Mother's Love

Only a mother's love
    is stronger than a child's cry
        in fear, blood, pain.

Only a mother's love
    holds her from despair,
        in shocked acceptance.

Any mother, anywhere,
    a Pakistani—this time—
        again and again, on a TV screen

From a makeshift clinic bed
    or bombed roadside rubble,
        a cry the same, in any language,

Consequence of atrocities
    that no cause of politics or war
        can make gain by such tragedy.

Only a mother's love
    lashed to the heart of not forgetting
        calls us to such witnessing.

2009

Our Time

What might have helped us mark
this corner of our time from dark?
In a world so rich in part, half starve,
bodies broken, hearts bled dry.

The course is problematical,
starvation mathematical.
Non-sleepers bawl, the keepers curse,
the have-nots steal, the haves hide purse.

Murmurs of war millions dead
say care for the future—everywhere,
yet hate shouts loud upon the stage
and love lies silent on the page.

1960s

Cascade of the Spirits

Thunderous force of Cascada Animas
creating earth's reservoir,
receives the shouts, the cries
of Gaia's children diving deep
into a pool of wondrous revelry.

2008, Chile

Spikes of Evergreens

How spikes of evergreens
   paint the sky
    orange, blue, and grey,

Pitchforks that bail
   sun's golden sheaves
    on cloud-high fields,

Shredding ribbons of cirrus,
   chasing dark trails
    of storm,

From uneven terrain, holding
   the last blushing crown
    of an ordinary day,

Their branching needles
   weave indigo blankets
    of night.

Evergreens, first apparitions
  to arise from morning's
    envelopment of fog,

Elegant and tall, uniformed
  sylvan coastal guards,
    sentinels of Puget Sound,

A regiment of rapiers,
  swords thrust toward
    a celestial dome,

Spires reaching
  for ancient meanings
    not yet understood.

2009

Lights Out

Might as well be midnight
    though only 6:45 p.m.

Winter solstice; planet
    turning out the light
    and my electrical switch
    does not respond.

Powerless, in disarray,
    dim flashlight, dull mind,
    I search for surfeit
    things to ease the loss.

Clever, until lights go out,
    the house grows cold,
    news, notes, accounts, to cope
    with the scope of life, undone.

Darkness comes too soon,
    the dinner uncooked,
    yet, in the garden,
    snow ghosts stray.

Profound in silences
    or whispering the wind,
    songs begin to stir
    my waning heart.

Peace steals into the drift,
the shutting down,
cuddled under blankets,
power to think, to dream:

Ancient fires, ancestors
kept bare skin warm
under bearskins, kept
warm without matches.

This dark winter's eve,
sky pale, opaque
on a far city veiled,
the world disappears.

Glad for paper and pen
to fill night's long hour,
I discover a gift of time
and a need for snow.

Too Much

Information comes and goes
    flows everywhere in languages
    enveloping the planet in
Excess of noise, cacophony;
    decibels of rage or calm,
    tones' magnetic waves
Bombarding atmosphere
    in clamorous overreach
    of channels cellular, and cells.
Information over mind,
    illusion of facts as reality,
    no subtle silences to end
All-inclusive macro sounds—
    too much to absorb,
    absolve, or comprehend.

2010

Candlelight

Not by light do I see
  but darkness in the space
    that flame allows—
      stranded after storm
      by failure of electric wire.

Wrapped in a blanket
  of silence, then flicker
    of heart in the night,
      a glow of mystery
      in oil and paraffin.

Pale wick of thought
  in flame's complexity,
    a perception of millennia,
      dark language of
      self's subtle knowing

That darkness holds
  dark matter and all
    the Universe together.

2007

350 ppm

I have found the power
to turn the world upside down,
see imagined heaven, make it earth,
overturning skies to green
in the clear image and atmosphere
of granny's crystal ball.

Set on a windowsill,
makes pure a cloudy yesterday,
orb that has no necessity
to weigh toxicity of molecules.

Friend's gift from his old granny
I never met, now surely dead,
soothsayer and spiritist
from knells of Derbyshire.

Unwrapped from a dark cloth,
the ball catches visions;
mind dances in light
of sentience, the psychic gift.

Phantom mists in crystal,
a drift of lifetimes sacrificed
for excesses of the few,
masks, pills, ventilators,
that neither ignorance nor
technology can save us from.

Come, gaze into the crystal ball
where the unanswered numbers
science gives, are clear—
We must reduce to 350 ppm
the CO_2 we breathe.

Or does it all come down to this—
our world turned upside down,
the future revealed
in the metaphor of a crystal ball?

PROMPTINGS

Epiphany

Sound—a strange shuffling force
near, yet far from context
of my reverie, a summer's reading
on a sunny afternoon, the porch
in peace and plenitude, and yet,
this infringement of atmosphere.

Beams that overhang the roof
appear the same, but in a windowpane,
reflected as a dream, the mirrored image
of a Great Blue Heron—
majestic against blue sky, standing
on the porch rail, legs long, alternately
balancing a breast robe of feathers,
neck a graceful curve.

I dare not move, dislodge
the skittish visitor, yet, slowly
turn my gaze full on
the proud prince of waterways—
inwardly crying, "Damn, no camera!"
My lost chance to be believed.

We'd met before, solitary creatures
at water's edge, our common knowledge
sand, rocks, gulls, a beach
where we test-step forward to each other,
step back, cautiously wait, until you fly,
but here on the porch I'm in your thrall,
in a moment's other-worldly way,
displacement in the power of a squawk.

I'm silenced by your pseudo-scream,
deep rasping, inscrutable in flight—
of the ancient order of Ciconiformes,
a silvered absence in the air.

We have met, but never as near,
on horizons of our unsure worlds,
you, now in surprise, I, under shadow
of porch roof—startled—when
a grand thud hits, then sounds
of scratching metal overhead.

Black talons, wrinkled tongs
seize the gutter above, flexing,
and I wait until an inch of golden beak
protrudes, moves slowly with exactitude
on bending neck,
until a curious eye catches its object,
knowing I was there.

Brash bird, I thought you'd gone,
taking whatever earthly warning
(or was it mine?) of this proverbial
kingdom—not human—not quite bird.
Your ancestors here long before mine,
and now, we've poisoned the water,
threatened your food and our own.

Both earthly creatures, vulnerable
on nature's chain. Have you come

to tell me what I cannot fathom
by human reasoning (being a creature
malformed, without wings)?

Have my eye and the eye of nature
met as harbinger—of what?
Sound of ruffling feathers,
wings release—heron gone.

But, three nights later, I stand
at the porch rail, watching the moon's
orange eye, its incisive light
an undulating shaft parting dark waters
—when straight as a winged arrow,
the Great Blue Heron flies by,
as if to mend our great divide.

2007

Ghosts

Green ghosts in summer palaces
  swing from rafters in the woods,
hold gold-leaved banners high
  to cerulean's gentle breeze.

Ghost songs creak in limbs
  as skies of pewter fall
through ochre sieves
  of gamboge and magenta.

Maple, oak, dispensing
  autumn's kaleidoscopic whirl
of umber lost in rustle,
  bare anatomy in drift.

Fallen on earth's clay shard,
  wind-lashed and fossilized,
rain-washed spines of sepia
  trace a fabulist's geology.

Connecticut

Poipu

The scene: a beach and rustling palms,
the star, a molting monk seal
opening one round, lugubrious eye
to frothy swirls of sand
and scant-clad bathers' revelry.

Warned: Caution! As if at the scene
of a crime, yellow tape surrounds
the slow moving seal, four hundred
pounds in ungainly lurch, that
yellow-vested volunteers safeguard.

Outrigger canoe, paddles splashing,
neophyte adventurers
embracing white-capped surf.
Breeze lifts bridal veil.
Bride in luster of silk,
holding stephanotis bouquet,
groom in tux, barefoot
they wade into the sea's
enfoldment of gold and emerald.

Returning outrigger
loses watery gain, until paddles
finally strike beach sand
and sun-drugged bathers
fold up the day in books and towels.

Slender bride leans low,
consoles a small bridesmaid,
the two poised like white egrets,
royal in solitary grace.

Seal thrusts fins with molting itch
and sand encrusted coat,
a camera eye on her,
blond lashes open,
then shutter of lens.
Eyes, her only beauty, now,
sad, sodden seal, longing for
the sinuous, watery world.

Photographer directs the kiss
of bride and bridegroom,
lining family under canopy.
A scent of meat upon a spit,
the drift of salty air
and life Hawaiian style.

At Poipu Beach Hotel,
seal reaches hedge barrier,
rubbing the back of her head
on a trailer wheel, she flounders
outrigger canoe in yellow tape.

Beach site, triumvirate,
disparity of three—
adventurers into the surf,
the perfect wedding scene,
and a molting monk seal
who dreams of birthing time.

2005, Kauai

Dream of the Barrios

Climb, Barrios, up dry mountains.
Your too many tin shacks
Crowd overburdened paths
With dreams of crystal fountains.

Below in the glass city
They have no clear insight how
To keep your mountains
From tumbling down one night,
And the scale is indifferent
That weighs one life against another
—except at the point of a knife.

So dream—of a gold watch
To stop time ticking against failure.
With a new pair of shoes
Walk down to the city's allure.
Dream of a body beautiful
Inheriting love, in a moment passing.
Dream-baby nine months more.

Dream—to stop your crying.
Round *arepas* are the ammunition
In hunger's daily war.
And robbery is in sweet pop
When thirst is for more, so pay!
Ice-cones melt your dreams away.

Climb, Barrios, up dry mountains
But don't risk the view,
Your wounds stream farther on horizons
Than anyone can dream.

1977, Caracas

Beggar Boy

You came upon me as I held
My purse to buy (what was it now?)
Cloying, with a voice
That was a whine.
"Déme, déme un Real."

Clever opportunist, why pick
This moment when I have packages to hold?
I resist on principle—
Having thought it over
A hundred times before—upon demand.

Wretched boy, don't you see
That I'm not able
To encourage such a style
By giving in and giving out
(What was it worth—a dime?)

That only makes you more the beggar,
I the fool, there must be
An alternative
To holding out a hand
For "Solo un Real."

Your face is not extraordinary.
I decide, on principle, to give you
Nothing, yet ever since,
Dark eyes on me, you claw
Into dull comforts of my life.

1976, Caracas

La Devorada

Miracle of baby flesh,
  no more than a photo
    in the morning news

Placed before us on the table
  with no one to blame
    but fate, and the effect

Of abject poverty
  and our indifference—
    the situation deplorable,

But we saw your case too late.
  Hunger already had devoured
    the child you might have been.

Footprints (of rats!)
  still scamper on the page
    your frail body opened

    Like rosebuds on the scene.

1976, Caracas

The Face of Another

At St. James entrance to the underground,
I am suddenly transported to a tropic isle—
by a glance, dark face, dark eyes that stare,
a woman who sits by the gateway there.

Why aren't you where the sea blows warm,
not here, in Seattle's cold light?
I could swear you are Lolita—
as you used to be, sitting on a porch
chatting with me, long years ago.

Lola, poet, friend, now brought to life—
the one who showed this macomber
(the one who comes across the waves)
Aruba's ways, her soul and seams,
the steel-drum bands and gospel tambourines.

Lola, friend of birthdays shared
of chocolate cake and 'Stacia yams,
of dances at the Windward Islands Club,
the dominoes and bingo hall, and all
the folk on Weg Fontin who let me in.

Caya Lolita E. Euson, street named
honoring you, Aruba's poet, my friend.
When did our long dialogue begin?

The day I stopped my car
and you passed by, your eyes on me,
asking "Have you lost direction?"
And I said "no," showing my painting
of a wooden shack, the colors red and blue
and curtains blowing out,
the house next door to yours.

"I always wished to paint," you said,
"but I write poetry instead."
And I replied that poems
were what I'd most like to do.

At the entrance to Seattle's underground
a woman stares and does not know
the effect of her eyes on me
as I scissor her face from the crowd,
mumbling "good morning," and
wondering how good a morning could be
with no place to go and nothing to see,
yet she offers me rich memory—
with the gift of her smile.

2003

Island Ever Home

Mango sun, magnet draws me on
to this shore, this feast at sunset hour

where golden sea shards shuffle in
and tropic breezes kiss the skin,
palms rustling tingles on the spine,
reviving life and love of another time
as falling waves dissolve, return
with each sand grain underfoot.

In this hour, a blindness of sun
nearing sea edge—taking the light.

2003, Aruba

High Tide

Bulkhead, barrier against high tide
  of days, years, anniversaries,
    moon's pull, storm's rage,
      seawall that keeps you far.

Seagulls, a pair, hunker
  then cry on wing, retrieving
    from stone-cracked shells
      succulence, and I dream.

Undertow of memories and molecules,
  night's dark liquidity,
    an iridescent flow of starfish,
      mollusks, sea kelp's sway.

White cresting manes, seahorses
  plunging deep in the briny kiss
    of waves, soothing shores of skin,
      rounding bays, inlets, high tide.

Vision

How ashes
　　turned crimson at the edge
　　of New Year's Eve,
　ashes black as night
　　surrounding fire.

Charred pages, words
　　of encouragement or grief
　　skittering on sand,
　fragile, breaking free
　　in disintegration—

　as if all ritual of years
　　had come to this.

31 December 2006

DEPARTURES

Journey

Couples, lovers, pairs,
old comfortables together
and I, a single traveler,
paddle with loose pen
toward imagined islands,
mainlands, elsewheres
in conscious drift.

Fabled life floundering
on barge, boat, sail,
sea sounds' incertitude,
listening for bones
of unembraceable words,
without you—entranced
by couples unmindful of
their gift, being together.

My ritual canoe swivels,
dips on tidal flow,
commanded by
an admiralty of one.

2005

Travel

You pulled the luggage of your life
 on wheels of time, through fog
  to leave me at the ferry dock,
your early morning shave
  soft lingering on my chin, a kiss,
   a hug, your passport held,
your mind and body leaving here
  as you walked down the plank—
   a passage too far to see.

2002

Pumpkin

Night black as goblin's garb,
  beach fire
bringing in old tides
  and the dory you restored,
painted the color of pumpkins
  with no rope to tow you in.

Five-horsepower chasing
  late-day reflections,
you, with fishing line
  —no fish—
on a boat called Pumpkin.

A flame seen afar
  on waters of Puget Sound
'til evening's color gone,
  and you ply home,
bucket and chain rigged,
  a pulley to haul her in,
bulkhead a resting bed.

This dark night
  we haul Pumpkin down,
pallbearers, setting fire.
  She burns in ancient ritual,
smoldering, brush and boards,
  then hiss and crackle,
flames licking floorboards,
  old bones blistering,
searing emotions release
  in ashes and sand.

Blue Glass

Sparkle of blue glass in sand
   that I reach for, but cannot find,
    blue, the color of your eyes,
washed smooth with stones,
   bronzed bits, bottles broken,
     opaque as our years together
      when we called this beach ours.

20 February 2010

Departing Art

You hang there—
    orphaned in dusky space,
walled up with other quadrants,
    art for art's sake.

From half a century's
    ritual dumping
of garbage at sunset
    into waters of Puget Sound,

Bits of tin, aluminum
    washed up on a beach,
dented, scrapped, for decades,
    all meaning in patina.

Gifts found one by one,
    fragments tossed, tattered,
edges honed, transformed
    on endless surge of tides,

Glinting in beach sand,
    deposited, returned,
arranged, painted, changed
    from dross to beauty.

Step-child of 'real art'
    set in a metal frame
to bring legitimacy,
    as if that might

Offer conduit of light
    to dazzle eyes,
give ripple of attention
    and help the loss

When each year another
    artful-child is hung
up for adoption
    at the Art Auction.

2008

Old Shirt, Old Pants

Abstraction of spattered paint
   on faded twill, threads worn bare
   to make repair, or remedy
   what time or negligence
   has put asunder.

Old shirt, elbow and cuff torn,
   stained dabs, smudges of color
   routing a map of years;
   the where and when
   of wielding paint and hammer.

Old pants raveled at the knee,
   not as today's fashion,
   but of grimy, humble work,
   grunt clothes that still hold
   a scent of sweat.

One body's energy
   manifest in tactile mobility
   of threads, slipping through fingers
   when pulled from a plastic bag,
   last remains to throw away.

2008, Cape Breton

When Evening Comes

When evening comes along the stairs
   in oblique rays of golden dust,
   I cannot tell if floating up
   or down, it seems to pause
   between tomorrow and the past
   but something flecks across the hall
   of memory and golden days.

I reach to pull the damask tight
   and at the windowpane I see
   that my old gate is still unlatched
   and nothing but wind grates it,
   or whispers on low grass
   or sweeps the dying leaves about.

The bare old oak with arms outspread
   entwines itself embracing sky,
   till embers of the afternoon
   fall grey and done with crackling games
   and my twin cats repair from sleep
   to hunt the land beyond my keep,
   I, from my window will attend
   the dying earth on her dark bed.

When evening comes along the stairs
   in slanting rays that reach the wall
   and at the corner disappear,
   I know I am alone.

1960s

Thread

So easily the silk thread
    slips from the needle's eye,
nothing of necessity
    to hold the garment
to its seams,
    nothing of precision
or memory to bind
    the finite cloth to light,
the dark magentas, purples
    fade—thread by silken thread,
a single life unraveling.

Chasm

What we both know—
the heart's rift—
a chasm between us
your eyes tell.

Paler than blue,
intensity dissolved
in space beyond
where I stand.

Pillowed on a bed
your rough face,
once beautiful,
creates a map

unique of years,
a fraction known,
contours fragile
I spread lotion on

hoping to warm
vitality, but you
have no requests
or accusals

though I seek clues
in your eyes
of imposed dimensions
you travel alone.

1998

Imprecision

At garden's edge, a barrier
  of white chrysanthemums,
    late afternoon
green-gold light flooding
  a spacious lawn
    where children and lovers
stray, and chrysanthemums
  soon kiss the evening air
    and fade with imprecision.

2010

My Darlings

A single leaf, unnoticed
  falls, a filament of molecules
  embedded in earth's scroll,
  her warp and weave.

The infants' fingers curl
  toward the twig, a branch
  on The Tree of Life,
  in a swirl of endless time.

One-hundred-sixty thousand years
  of birth, joy, pain, and death,
  child, the infinitesimal seed
  of five thousand generations

Assembling and disassembling,
  becoming the dream
  of providence and peace
  in release of semen and egg.

Love's seminal, sacred deed,
  claim of inheritance,
  blood, the placental veil lifted
  to light and consciousness.

Each child a holographic universe
  transforming tides of birth,
  place, politics, and entropy—
  the force of life surviving

To flourish under yellow skies,
   or float in brine of glacial melt,
   particles of CO_2, or nuclear debris.
   Do we, the living, understand

How high on fragile limbs
   of useless wars and broken promises
   we are, for lack of languages to give
   meaning to minds opening?

Divergent, converging souls
   wake from planetary sleep,
   shifting thought, wary that
   arrogance cuts down the tree.

The unborn depend on us
   more than we know—to hear
   primal songs of ancestral memory
—and their longing to become...

Oh, my darlings, are you there
                —for the future?

Space Stone

Here I am—worrying about the Moon—
    Why on Earth
    Worry about the Moon?

Yet, in a dream, words unbidden come:
    Space Stone
    Stone Space

What meaning such a vision—
    Ether or
    Solidity?

Ambiguity of view, sigh, song.
    Moon face
    Night anchor

Sun's reflected light, the cosmic eye
    Science and Myth
    Entwined

Ancient histories, fear's dark side
    Waxing, waning
    Seascape's tide

I dream of the Moon (and maybe Mars)
    Spacecraft of entrepreneurs
    Ax, ice, planted flags

Strategic Control
    Rare earth elements
    War or survival?

I dream of the Moon (and maybe Mars)
    Space Stone
    Stone Space

What entities—out there—
    Will dream us and wonder
    What happened here?

Transforming Time

Was it Wednesday, or some Thursday,
when I met you
walking tarmac to a plane
bound for Zurich—or someplace,
maybe Qantas to Sydney,
or the old Pan Am,
but, because of a brilliant sun,
it must have been Australian
sands shifting on Bondi Beach,
I, blinded by chance, being there,
but not sure, you running
sure-footed in the moment when
I wondered, why am I here?

But it is you, now,
remembrance only, left in time,
while I feel the dry
Nebraska earth under my feet,
my head high in worldly visions
when you came walking in,
sifting one country from another,
fast—though time runs slow,
experiencing—stretching beyond
what I imagined, growing up
in kindergarten games.

Spot and Dick and Jane,
my stockings falling down,
books falling from shelves,
catsup exploding on painted walls,
head cracked, flying from a swing
failing to hold on, and an audience
not hearing the song
of a robin with clipped wings.
Caught in confusion
of galloping horses—I was
too hoarse to sing.

Now, flying everywhere,
carrying a burning fire,
I sight ancestral bones, images,
mirage of millennial seas
where time has no shore and lives
bleed into the unfolding
manifest of minds,
swift in lightness of light,
the weightlessness of being.

2013

Arrival

Flight into the eternal now,
  velocity of spirit flowing
    in quantum complexity
      of galaxies, star seeds, entities
        from random nano-sparks
          caught in sun's celestial light
          and the gravity of time,
          one small wail in history,
          a child arrives, unfolding
          from cell's invention,
        inimitable, infinite, surviving
      the thrust of life, the ethereal
    interval between the blink and flash
of the I Am, we are.

2009

Step Over The Boundary

Step over the boundary of self into the universe
Where the skin of self
Is known as wind perfume.
Its fragrance, a message in poetry.

Winds of harsh pain are caught
In the onslaught of mind's
Presumptions of physical reality.

Standing in flames, arrows of desire, unable
To step beyond emotion's pain, chains of mind
Bind this body to its pain,
That love considered, that is self-love.

Spent arrows of desire miss
The harvest of intent, the gathering in.
I must learn (I must) that all thoughts
Strike elsewhere, beyond
The farthest boundaries of my intent.

Flesh of self desiring
Taut bow drawn across the body's pain,
Release in arrow's shaft
This life's experiences with love.
Release, let fall beyond the visceral
Contingencies of one small life.

Release beyond the boundary of time
Thought form into energy,
This one body's universe
Into an ever unfolding universe
Beyond whatever arrows spent,
The thrust of small thoughts enjoin
Celestial rhythms of the universe.

Feel earth's beat in the heart of now.
Understand the message of the wind.
Learn from the storm in storm's aftermath.
Release inner self to being.
Stones fall into tears.

Step over the boundary of self
Into the embrace of the universe.

...received as automatic writing
1987
Skidmore College, International Women Writers Conference

Spirit Journey Books was created when my husband and I
returned from a trip to China and I self-published
my first book. We lived on Dolphin Beach
on the island of Vashon,
near Seattle, Washington.

The Dolphin – mythological communicator of the deep,
revered helper of humans, especially at sea –
is now endangered.
The spiral symbolizes non-linear time
expanding through perception and imagination.

When did I start writing poems?
As a child, with my doggerel,
decorating birthday cards for my parents.
I always drew and painted.
As an adult, traveling and living in foreign places,
I longed for words to describe what I saw and felt,
and I began to write.

Born and raised in Lincoln, Nebraska,
I have lived on four continents and two islands.
For the last quarter century, I have resided on
Vashon Island in the state of Washington.
A member of Valise Art Gallery,
I also sing with the Threshold choir.
Poet laureate of Vashon Island for 2013–2015,
I continue to write stories and poems and create art.